S0-CIF-078

THE **REAL** STORY:
DEBUNKING HISTORY

THE REAL STORY BEHIND THE

FOUNDING FATHERS

RACHAEL MORLOCK

PowerKiDS press

New York

Published in 2020 by The Rosen Publishing Group, Inc.
29 East 21st Street, New York, NY 10010

Copyright © 2020 by The Rosen Publishing Group, Inc.

All rights reserved. No part of this book may be reproduced in any form without permission in writing from the publisher, except by a reviewer.

First Edition

Editor: Jill Keppeler
Book Design: Reann Nye

Photo Credits: Cover https://commons.wikimedia.org/wiki/File:Declaration_of_Independence_(1819),_by_John_Trumbull.jpg; p. 5 Courtesy of the Library of Congress; p. 7 Stock Montage/Archive Photos/Getty Images; p. 8 https://commons.wikimedia.org/wiki/File:John_Adams_(1766).jpg; p. 9 https://commons.wikimedia.org/wiki/File:Writing_the_Declaration_of_Independence_1776_cph.3g09904.jpg; p. 11 PHAS/Universal Images Group/Getty Images; p. 13 https://upload.wikimedia.org/wikipedia/commons/1/18/Mrs_James_Warren_%28Mercy_Otis%29%2C_by_John_Singleton_Copley.jpg; pp. 14, 15, 29 Bettmann/Getty Images; p. 17 (top) Historical/Cobis Historical/Getty Images; p. 17 (bottom) https://commons.wikimedia.org/wiki/File:Gilbert_Stuart_Williamstown_Portrait_of_George_Washington.jpg; p. 18 https://commons.wikimedia.org/wiki/File:Treaty_of_Paris_1783_-_last_page_(hi-res).jpg; p. 19 De Agostini Picture Library/De Agostini/Getty Images; p. 21 (top) https://commons.wikimedia.org/wiki/File:Scene_at_the_Signing_of_the_Constitution_of_the_United_States.jpg; p. 21 (bottom) https://commons.wikimedia.org/wiki/File:Benjamin_Franklin_Signature.svg; p. 23 Photo Josse/Leemage/Corbis Historical/Getty Images; p. 25 (left) https://commons.wikimedia.org/wiki/File:An_Advertisement_of_The_Federalist_-_Project_Gutenberg_eText_16960.jpg; p. 25 (right) https://commons.wikimedia.org/wiki/File:JamesMadison.jpg; p. 27 GraphicaArtis/Archive Photos/Getty Images.

Cataloging-in-Publication Data

Names: Morlock, Rachael.
Title: The real story behind the founding fathers / Rachael Morlock.
Description: New York : PowerKids Press, 2020. | Series: The real story: debunking history | Includes glossary and index.
Identifiers: ISBN 9781538344620 (pbk.) | ISBN 9781538343432 (library bound) | ISBN 9781538344637 (6pack)
Subjects: LCSH: Founding Fathers of the United States–Juvenile literature. | United States–History–Revolution, 1775-1783–Juvenile literature.
Classification: LCC E302.5 M67 2020 | DDC 973.3–dc23

Manufactured in the United States of America

CPSIA Compliance Information: Batch #CSPK19. For Further Information contact Rosen Publishing, New York, New York at 1-800-237-9932

CONTENTS

THE WHOLE TRUTH

American history is often told through stories of its leaders. Many of the leaders from the time of the Revolutionary War are known as the Founding Fathers of the United States. They shaped the most important events of that period. As a group, they declared America's independence, fought in the war for freedom, and created a new national government. The Founding Fathers include George Washington, John Adams, Thomas Jefferson, James Madison, John Jay, Alexander Hamilton, and Benjamin Franklin.

Today, the Founding Fathers are often more like myths than men. Stories about these American heroes are often made-up or incomplete. As Benjamin Franklin wrote, "Half the truth is often a great lie." The real stories of the Founding Fathers can only be found by looking beyond the half-truths passed down throughout history.

LEADERS AND FOLLOWERS

Any list of the Founding Fathers must leave out many people. The Declaration of Independence was signed by 56 **delegates**. The Constitution was signed by 39. The Continental army was made up of about 231,000 men over the course of the war, including African Americans and Native Americans. Women played an important role in the changes underway, although they weren't represented in the founding events. The Founding Fathers are remembered by history, but they never acted alone.

Paintings of the Founding Fathers decorate
the National Archives. There, visitors can view
important **documents** that shaped the United
States—the Declaration of Independence, the U.S.
Constitution, and the Bill of Rights.

REVOLUTIONARY RUMBLINGS

It's easy to believe that the Founding Fathers were a united group with one goal—but that's not totally true. A new union had sprung up between the colonies as they shared complaints against the British. Still, there were many issues that the colonists disagreed on. Within and between colonies, there was a wide range of opinions about the best way to fight England's **injustice**.

Delegates from 12 of the 13 colonies took part in the Continental Congress that started in 1774. Even members of the Continental Congress disagreed about how to act. Many wanted to keep their ties to England instead of breaking away as an independent country. They argued about this even after the Revolutionary War had begun. A declaration of independence was far from certain.

PAUL REVERE'S RIDE

In 1861, Henry Wadsworth Longfellow wrote a poem about Paul Revere's night ride. The poem **exaggerated** Revere's actions. It extended the two-hour ride to last through the night. It also left out other riders who traveled to deliver the message. In reality, Revere made it to Lexington, but he failed to reach Concord, Massachusetts, because the British stopped him. Another rider, Samuel Prescott, made it through to warn Concord.

FACT FINDER

Americans weren't united in the Revolution. After the war began, about 50,000 colonists fought alongside the British. They were called Loyalists. Towns and cities were divided between Loyalists and new American patriots.

The Revolutionary War began on the morning of April 19, 1775, in Lexington, Massachusetts. Paul Revere famously raced on horseback the night before to warn patriots that the British were coming.

DECLARING INDEPENDENCE

It's easy to forget how undecided the Founding Fathers and the Continental Congress were at this time. They were enthusiastic about the rights of Americans, but they weren't ready to stand on their own as a country. By early summer 1776, more than a year had passed since the Revolutionary War started—but the Continental Congress was still **debating** about whether to declare independence.

Members of the Continental Congress began their final debate over independence on July 1, 1776. The next day, 12 of the 13 colonies voted for independence. (New York had not yet been given permission by its government to vote on the issue.) The date was July 2, 1776. John Adams wrote a letter to his wife **predicting** that the day would be remembered and joyfully celebrated by future Americans.

JOHN ADAMS

Five delegates were assigned the task of writing a declaration of independence. Benjamin Franklin, John Adams, and Thomas Jefferson are shown in this painting.

THE FOURTH OF JULY

Adams was partly right. The games, parades, and festivities that he predicted have come to mark Independence Day, but not on that date. The Continental Congress declared independence from England on July 2, but on July 4, it approved the Declaration of Independence, which explained the reasons for the decision. It's this day that's most remembered by history.

There was no one day of monumental change and celebration. News of independence spread slowly. The city of Philadelphia celebrated sooner than most. George Washington and the Continental army heard of the great event July 9. The news didn't reach some of the colonies for several weeks. The British government in London did not receive the Declaration of Independence until August 30, nearly two months later.

THE SIGNING

Only two people signed the original Declaration of Independence on July 4, 1776: Continental Congress president John Hancock and secretary Charles Thomson. After New York finally voted for independence on July 9, 1776, Congress had a special copy of the declaration made. Starting August 2, the signers put their names to it as they arrived for work over the next few days. One delegate, Thomas McKean, didn't sign it until the next year.

On July 4, 1776, Philadelphia celebrated by holding a citywide party and public readings of the Declaration of Independence.

"REMEMBER THE LADIES"

You know about the Founding Fathers—but few people ever mention "Founding Mothers." All 56 signers of the Declaration of Independence were men. They spoke for the women of the United States as well. These women weren't silent, but history rarely remembers them.

In 1776, Abigail Adams sent a letter to her husband, John Adams. As he laid the foundation for a new nation, she asked him to "Remember the Ladies." Abigail warned that women "will not hold ourselves bound by any Laws in which we have no voice, or Representation."

Alongside men, women such as Abigail Adams secured American independence with their intelligence, hard work, and sacrifice. However, the Founding Fathers didn't extend political equality to women. They disregarded Abigail's strong, clear words and the contributions of many other women.

FACT FINDER

One story tells that, during the war, British general Charles Cornwallis or one of his men said: "We may destroy all the men in America, and we shall still have all we can do to defeat the women."

Mercy Otis Warren was a writer who
influenced the American public with her
political poems, plays, and histories.
She sent frequent letters to the founders
expressing her views on government.

BETSY ROSS'S FLAG

Betsy Ross is one of the few women who appears in stories of the Revolution. According to the legend, she was a seamstress in Philadelphia. One day in 1776, the story goes, George Washington and other men came to Ross's shop with a design, and she agreed to make the first American flag.

However, there is no proof that this story is true. Ross really was a seamstress in Philadelphia. It's clear from her shop records that she sewed and was paid for many flags during the Revolutionary War. Whether she made the first flag is unclear. The story became popular in 1870, nearly a century later, when her grandson told the family tale to the Historical Society of Pennsylvania. Since then, Ross's name has become deeply woven into American history.

BETSY ROSS

In the story Betsy Ross's grandson told, she suggested changing the stars on Washington's flag design from six-point stars to five-point stars. Ross showed him her star-making method, the story says, and Washington agreed.

WAGING WAR

George Washington became famous for commanding the Continental army during the Revolutionary War. But contrary to his popular image today, Washington's military record was far from perfect. His mistakes as a young leader helped start the French and Indian War. Washington lost more battles than he won in the Revolutionary War, but his creativity and leadership led the army to victory in the overall conflict.

A **fictional** story tells that Washington chopped down a cherry tree as a boy. The story says he then admitted it to his father, saying, "I cannot tell a lie." These ideals, however, didn't apply to his actions in war. Washington organized a highly successful spy ring and was particularly good at sneaking up on or away from his enemies. As a military leader, Washington's actions were tricky and unpredictable.

GEORGE WASHINGTON

Washington was very tall for his time. Instead of wearing a wig like most men of the day, Washington powdered his own long, reddish hair to make it look white. The story of Washington's wooden teeth has been passed down through the years. In fact, Washington had several sets of uncomfortable false teeth in his life, but none were wooden. Most were made with ivory or cow, human, or horse teeth.

FACT FINDER

The Culper Ring was made up of ordinary citizens and military members. They sent secret information using codes and invisible ink. They also helped spread false rumors started by Washington.

Washington sent Nathan Hale over enemy lines as a spy. After Hale was captured and killed, Washington created a better operation. He organized spies in the Culper Ring.

< GEORGE WASHINGTON

PEACE AT LAST

On October 19, 1781, the British surrendered to George Washington's army of American and French forces at the Battle of Yorktown. The war had raged for six years, and the American victory at Yorktown is often considered the end of the Revolutionary War.

However, although Yorktown was the last land battle, fighting continued at sea for the next few years. American ships, as well as ships from the Netherlands and Spain, battled English ships on the high seas and limited English trade.

The war on land and sea officially ended in 1783. John Adams, Benjamin Franklin, and John Jay went to Paris to set the terms of peace with England. The resulting Treaty of Paris set up America's future as an independent country.

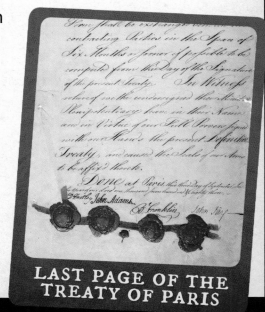

LAST PAGE OF THE TREATY OF PARIS

Adams, Franklin, and Jay all signed the
Treaty of Paris. The treaty outlined America's
boundaries, sorted out money issues, and set
fair treatment of Loyalists in America.

CREATING THE CONSTITUTION

After the war, the United States faced the challenge of creating a just and effective government. The first constitution wasn't the one we have now. The Founding Fathers' first attempt, the Articles of Confederation, wasn't a success. In 1787, the Constitutional Convention gathered—not to write a new constitution but to improve the Articles of Confederation. However, this quickly changed.

Not everyone was pleased by the convention. Some disagreed with its goals from the beginning. Rhode Island objected and chose not to participate. The remaining 12 states sent representatives to protect their interests in the new government. However, although the states chose 74 delegates, only 55 took part in the convention. Even when the U.S. Constitution was complete, three of the 42 delegates present that day refused to sign the document.

BENJAMIN FRANKLIN'S
SIGNATURE ∨

∧ Benjamin Franklin
is one of only six
people who signed
both the Declaration
of Independence
of the Constitution.
Jefferson appears in
this painting of the
convention, although
he was in France
during that time.

SIDESTEPPING SLAVERY

The Founding Fathers are famous for standing for freedom—but this didn't apply to freedom for all Americans. They missed an opportunity to abolish, or do away with, slavery in the new government they formed. The Declaration of Independence contains the phrase "All men are created equal," but that notion was missing from the Constitution.

Washington, Jefferson, Madison, Franklin, and Jay were slave owners. Although Washington freed his slaves in his will and Jay was actually an **abolitionist** who freed his slaves gradually, these men and other founders used slave labor to keep their estates running. Adams and Hamilton strongly objected to slavery, and Franklin became an abolitionist later. One of the greatest failings of the Founding Fathers, however, was that they left the problem of slavery for later generations to tackle.

FREEDOM FOR SOME

It may be surprising that the leaders who risked so much for their own liberty continued to **oppress** others. They failed to protect the rights of African Americans, American Indians, and women, even though members of all three groups joined the struggle for independence. The Founding Fathers' idea that government was meant to protect "life, liberty, and the pursuit of happiness" didn't apply to all Americans.

Washington's slaves kept his home, Mount Vernon, running. Of the first five presidents, Adams was the only one who didn't own slaves. Adams believed the American Revolution was incomplete without freedom for slaves.

RATIFICATION

While the U.S. Constitution is respected today, not every state was happy with it early on. After the convention, the Constitution still had to be ratified, or approved, by the states. Five states quickly did so. The remaining states debated about the document. Some people fought it! Many opponents thought it gave the federal government too much power. They wanted to see more protections for the rights of the people.

Alexander Hamilton, John Jay, and James Madison set out to persuade people to support the Constitution. They **anonymously** wrote "The Federalist Papers," a set of 85 essays explaining the Constitution. Still, several states refused to ratify without a list of rights. Even though Madison had been opposed to the idea, he took on the task of outlining the basic rights of the American people.

FACT FINDER

Madison used ideas from the states, the Virginia Declaration of Rights, and other sources to write 19 amendments. These were gradually narrowed down to the 10 amendments in the Bill of Rights.

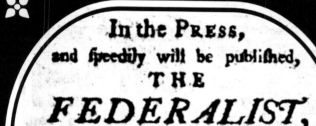

In the **PRESS**,
and speedily will be published,
THE
FEDERALIST,
A Collection of Essays written in favor of the New Constitution.
By a Citizen of New-York.
Corrected by the Author, with Additions and Alterations.

This work will be printed on a fine Paper and good Type, in one handsome Volume duodecimo, and delivered to subscribers at the moderate price of one dollar. A few copies will be printed on superfine royal writing paper, price ten shillings.

No money required till delivery.

To render this work more complete, will be added, without any additional expence,

PHILO-PUBLIUS,
AND THE

Madison realized that adding a list of rights was key to ratifying the Constitution. He later became the fourth president of the United States.

ADVERTISEMENT FOR
THE FEDERALIST,
A COLLECTION OF
"THE FEDERALIST PAPERS"

RELIGIOUS FREEDOM

Within the Bill of Rights, the First Amendment promises freedom of religion. It forbids the government from **dictating** religious practices. Though the Founding Fathers clearly valued religious freedom, however, people are sometimes confused about the Founding Fathers' individual beliefs.

Many claim that the Founding Fathers were all Christians. Others say that they were Deists, members of a movement popular at the time. Deism values reason, and holds that there is one God who's present in nature but doesn't interact with humans. The two belief systems may also blend. In truth, the beliefs of the Founding Fathers were deeply personal, often private, and changed throughout their lives. Their backgrounds likely mean they were sometimes **motivated** by Christian morals and beliefs. However, they used the Bill of Rights to protect religious practices from the influence of the federal government.

FACT FINDER

Although the Declaration of Independence refers to "Nature's God" and the "Creator," there is no mention of God in the Constitution.

Ben Franklin was a famous supporter of religious tolerance. Franklin was a Deist, but he also gave money to a number of religious organizations in Philadelphia.

FRIENDS AND RIVALS

The great achievements of the Founding Fathers create an impression of a close team of leaders. However, although they sometimes shared important friendships, they also fell into frequent and heated arguments. They were often openly **critical** of each other's personalities, ideas, and partnerships. Disagreements among the Founding Fathers led to the creation of different political parties.

Jefferson and Adams were friends and rivals. Their friendship began at the Continental Congress and lasted until they both ran for president in 1800. The election and the transfer of presidential power from Adams to Jefferson ruined their bond until about 1811. With time, the two leaders were able to restore their friendship and wrote frequent letters to each other. They died just hours apart on the same day: July 4, 1826.

Alexander Hamilton was killed in a duel with his fellow lawyer and political rival, Aaron Burr. Hamilton was well known for his short temper and strong opinions.

THE REAL FOUNDING FATHERS

Over time, the sharp personalities of the Founding Fathers have been smoothed over. Heroic figures have replaced the real men who were both visionary and wise—and short sighted and hot tempered. Forgetting the flaws of the Founding Fathers means losing sight of the story of their accomplishments and failures as ordinary men.

The Founding Fathers shaped a new country in a time of great uncertainty, danger, and disagreement. Their ideas weren't always popular, and they had to act with certainty at a time when America's future was far from secure. Myths and stories fall short in showing how slow and difficult the process of building a nation was for the founding generations of Americans. If you look beyond these tales, you can glimpse the real lives and challenges of the Founding Fathers.

GLOSSARY

abolitionist: A person fighting to end slavery.

anonymous: Not named.

critical: Expressing disapproval.

debate: An argument or public discussion, or to have an argument or public discussion.

delegate: A person sent to a meeting or convention to represent others.

dictate: To give orders.

document: A formal piece of writing.

exaggerate: To enlarge a fact or statement beyond what is true.

fictional: Being a made-up story.

injustice: An unfair or bad act.

motivate: To be a reason for something or to give someone a reason for doing something.

oppress: To unjustly use power over another.

predict: To guess what will happen in the future based on facts.

INDEX

WEBSITES

Due to the changing nature of Internet links, PowerKids Press has developed an online list of websites related to the subject of this book. This site is updated regularly. Please use this link to access the list: www.powerkidslinks.com/debunk/fathers